FAMOUS FIGURES OF

JESSE JAMES

THE AMERICAN FRONTIER

FAMOUS FIGURES OF THE AMERICAN FRONTIER

FAMOUS FIGURES OF
JESSE JAMES
THE AMERICAN FRONTIER

Barbara Saffer

Chelsea House Publishers
Philadelphia

Produced for Chelsea House by
OTTN Publishing, Stockton, NJ

CHELSEA HOUSE PUBLISHERS
Editor in Chief: Sally Cheney
Associate Editor in Chief: Kim Shinners
Production Manager: Pamela Loos
Art Director: Sara Davis
Series Designer: Keith Trego

First Printing

1 3 5 7 9 8 6 4 2

The Chelsea House World Wide Web address is
http://www.chelseahouse.com

Library of Congress Cataloging-in-Publication Data

Saffer, Barbara.
Jesse James / by Barbara Saffer
    p.   cm. – (Famous figures of the American frontier)
Includes bibliographical references and index.
    ISBN 0-7910-6499-9 (alk. paper)
    ISBN 0-7910-6500-6 (pbk.: alk. paper)
1. James, Jesse, 1847-1882–Juvenile literature. 2. Outlaws–
West (U.S.)–Biography–Juvenile literature. 3. Frontier and
pioneer life–West (U.S.)–Juvenile literature. 4. West (U.S.)–
History–1860-1890–Juvenile literature. [James, Jesse, 1847-
1882. 2. Robbers and outlaws. 3. Frontier and pioneer
life–West (U.S.). 4. West (U.S.)–History.] I. Title. II. Series.

F594.J27 S24 2001
364.1'55'092–dc21   2001028863

CONTENTS

The life and death of the famous outlaw Jesse James remain shrouded in mystery. Some people feel the famous outlaw did not die in 1882, as is commonly believed. In 1995, scientists exhumed Jesse's body and performed DNA tests on the remains, hoping to put the legend of Jesse James to rest once and for all.

The Legend of
Jesse James

In the fall of 1881, Jesse James was tired of running from the law. He had been an *outlaw* for 16 years. Using the name Thomas Howard, the bandit rented a house in St. Joseph, Missouri, where he lived with his wife, Zee, and their two children, Jesse Jr. and Mary. The small house was on a hill with an excellent view, so Jesse could see enemies approaching from any direction. The outlaw was always ready to make a quick getaway at the first sign of trouble.

Jesse James had good reason to be *vigilant*. Missouri's governor, Thomas Crittenden, was determined to get rid of Jesse and his gang. The governor called on the citizens of Missouri to chase the bandits "by day or by night, until the entire band is either captured or exterminated." As an incentive, Crittenden offered a $10,000 reward.

Two members of the James Gang, Bob and Charlie Ford, could not resist the huge bounty. In spring 1882, the Ford brothers were staying at Jesse James's house while the gang planned a bank robbery. After breakfast on April 3, Jesse and the Fords stepped into the parlor to discuss the heist. Jesse was always well-armed and watchful, even with his *accomplices*. That morning, however, Jesse made a fatal mistake. He took off his guns, laid them down, and climbed onto a chair to straighten and dust a picture. As soon as Jesse's back was turned, Bob Ford raised his gun and shot Jesse in the head.

The blast brought Jesse's wife and children running into the room. The Fords told Zee James that a pistol had accidentally gone off, then raced out to telegraph the governor. America's best-known

Jesse James is shot in the back of the head by Bob Ford in this illustration from an early book on the outlaw's life. Years later James R. Ross, the great-grandson of Jesse James, recalled: "My grandfather told me he ran into the house and saw his father lying on the floor with a bullet in his head and blood running out. All his life, my grandfather remembered that day."

outlaw, 34 years old, lay dead on the floor.

Jesse James's body was removed by law enforcement officials and examined by doctors. The body was then released to Zee James, who accompanied it to Jesse's hometown of Kearney, Missouri. While the family arranged his funeral, Jesse's body lay in the Kearney Hotel. There, hundreds of people—including Jesse's family, friends, supporters, and foes—saw it. No one who knew Jesse doubted that the body was actually that of Jesse James.

When word got out that someone had murdered Jesse James, many people were shocked and outraged. "The Ballad of Jesse James" soon spread throughout the country. Here are a few verses:

He robbed from the rich
    and was a friend to the poor;
He had a heart and a hand and a brain.
With his brother Frank,
    he robbed the Northfield bank
And stopped the Glendale train.

The people held their breath,
    when they heard of Jesse's death
And wondered how he ever came to die;
It was one of the gang,
    called little Robert Ford,
He shot poor Jesse on the sly.

Poor Jesse had a wife
    to mourn for his life
Three children, they were brave,
But that dirty little coward
    that shot Mister Howard,
Has laid poor Jesse in his grave.

Some people, however, refused to believe the famous outlaw was dead. They insisted that Jesse had faked his death. During the next few years, many men claimed to be the "real" Jesse James. These assertions were denied by the James family. Even today, though, unrelated people claim to be descendants of Jesse James.

To end questions about Jesse's death, his Missouri grave was opened in 1995. The body was studied by experts, then reburied. The remains corresponded with known features of Jesse James, and the body's DNA matched that of living members of the James family. Thus, scientists concluded that Jesse James truly was killed in 1882.

Nonetheless, there is still controversy surrounding the famous villain. In 1951, J. Frank Dalton, an old man living in Granbury, Texas, claimed to be Jesse James. He died soon afterward and was buried under a tombstone that reads "Jesse Woodson James." It includes the inscription "Supposedly killed in 1882." Most historians and scientists dismiss Dalton's claim. Some Granbury residents, however, believe it is true. They wanted to have DNA tests performed on Dalton's remains. However, when Dalton's grave was *exhumed*, his body was not in it. The man buried there was of a different age and was missing an arm. It was believed that because of an error in the cemetery records, the headstone had been set on the wrong grave. Thus, the saga of Jesse James continues.

Well before his death in 1882, Jesse James was a legend. His famous exploits—including bank, train, and stagecoach robberies—were *blazoned* in newspaper articles, songs, books, stories, and plays. Despite his lawless actions and *infamy* as a bandit, Jesse James became a folk hero.

A painting of Jesse James, made from a famous photograph of the outlaw at a young age. By the time Jesse James was 16, he had started on a life of violence.

THE EARLY YEARS

In 1842, Robert Sallee James and his wife Zerelda Cole James left their native Kentucky and moved to Clay County in western Missouri. The young couple bought a farm near the town of Kearney, and Robert, a Baptist minister, became pastor of the New Hope Baptist Church. Like many farmers who migrated from the South, the Jameses owned black slaves.

Robert and Zerelda's first child, Frank, was born on January 10, 1843. A second son, Robert, died in infancy. Their third son, Jesse Woodson James, was born on September 5, 1847, and a daughter, Susan, arrived on November 25, 1849.

By 1850, the California gold rush was in full swing. Robert James decided to go west to preach to the *prospectors* and perhaps strike gold himself. Shortly after he reached California, Robert died of *pneumonia*. In 1852, Zerelda married a wealthy farmer named Benjamin Simms. Simms did not get along with Frank and Jesse James, though. A divorce was planned, but Simms suddenly died. In 1855, Zerelda married a doctor named Reuben Samuel. The union was a happy one, and Reuben and Zerelda had four children of their own: Archie, John, Sallie, and Fannie.

Like many youngsters, Frank and Jesse James worked on the family farm, attended school, went to church, and played with friends. By 1854, however, western Missouri was racked by conflict. The neighboring territories of Kansas and Nebraska were being settled, and the residents would be allowed to vote on the issue of slavery. The struggle between supporters and opponents of slavery was fierce.

Zerelda James Samuel is pictured behind her two famous sons. Jesse is on the right and Frank on the left in this tintype.

Proslavery leaders brought in settlers that favored slavery, and *abolitionist* leaders recruited settlers that opposed slavery. The area became a deadly combat zone, with fierce fighting between anti-slavery and proslavery factions.

Jesse James's family lived in Missouri's border region, near the Kansas boundary. Most border residents approved of slavery, and many local men formed *guerrilla* bands to raid abolitionist towns in Kansas. The guerrillas struck suddenly, robbing, murdering, and burning property, then escaped into the woods, or bush. They were nicknamed *bushwhackers*. Abolitionist raiders, who were called *jayhawkers*, did the same thing by attacking towns and communities where slavery was supported. As a result, Frank and Jesse James grew up surrounded by brutality and death.

In November 1860, Abraham Lincoln was elected president of the United States. Because Lincoln was an opponent of slavery, many of the Southern states decided to *secede* from the Union. They formed a new government, the Confederate States of America. This led to the Civil War between the Union (North) and the Confederacy (South). Though the state of Missouri remained loyal to the Union, many people living on the southern border–including Jesse James's family–supported the South. Guerrillas from the border region fought for the Confederacy to protect their property and way of life. In 1862, at the age of 18, Frank James joined a guerrilla troop led by William Quantrill.

Quantrill's force, called Quantrill's Raiders, was a ferocious band of bushwhackers that struck quickly and viciously. They attacked Union camps and supply wagons, ambushed patrols, burned bridges, and cut telegraph lines. They killed soldiers and pro-Union civilians alike, robbed stores and banks, and destroyed homes and businesses. Quantrill's Raiders sometimes hid on the James-Samuel farm, and Jesse came to know them well. One of Quantrill's men whom Jesse befriended was named Cole Younger.

Zerelda Samuel was a strong supporter of the Confederate cause. She collected information about Union troops and gave it to Jesse, who sneaked it to local guerrilla bands.

On May 25, 1863, Union soldiers invaded the James-Samuel farm. Finding Jesse plowing a field, they lashed him with a whip. The soldiers then forced their way into the house and demanded information about Frank James and his guerrilla troop. Jesse's mother and step-

Frank James recalled: "I will never forget the first time I ever saw Quantrill. He was nearly six feet in height, rather thin, his hair and moustache was sandy and he was full of life and a jolly fellow. He had none of the air of the bravado or the *desperado* about him ... he was a demon in battle." William Quantrill is pictured above.

father refused to answer, so the soldiers dragged Dr. Samuel outside and hung him from a tree. The soldiers pulled Dr. Samuel up and down three times, nearly strangling him. The doctor was frightened into revealing that Frank's unit was hiding in the woods near the house. The Union troops surprised the bushwhackers, took their clothing, horses, and stolen loot, and killed some of them. Many of the guerrillas, including Frank, got away. Jesse was just 15 years old, but he swore he would get even.

In addition to harassing Confederate supporters, Union troops sometimes jailed them to keep them

This *Harper's Magazine* illustration shows the aftermath of the attack on Lawrence, Kansas, by Quantrill's Raiders in August 1863.

from aiding the enemy. On August 14, 1863, a three-story warehouse in Kansas City, used to house women prisoners, collapsed. The victims included two sisters of Bill Anderson, one of Quantrill's officers. A few days later, on August 18, General Thomas C. Ewing, a Union officer, ordered all Confederate sympathizers to leave the Missouri border area. Thousands of men, women, and children were forced from their homes. Union troops then marched through the region, demolishing everything in their path. The soldiers destroyed crops, tore down fences, burned farms, and killed livestock. The displaced citizens included the families of some of Quantrill's followers.

Quantrill and his supporters were **incensed** by these events, and they wanted revenge. They decided to raid Lawrence, Kansas, an abolitionist stronghold. At dawn on August 21, 1863, William Quantrill, Bill Anderson, Frank James, Cole Younger, and a force of about 450 guerrillas charged into Lawrence. The bushwhackers raced through the streets, screaming and firing their guns. The raiders killed men and boys, shot horses, and burned property. At least 150 people were murdered in the savage guerrilla raid. Bill Anderson

killed with such fury and relish that he became
known as "Bloody Bill Anderson." Afterward,
Governor Thomas Carney of Kansas wrote, "No
fiends in human shape could have acted with more
savage barbarity than did Quantrill and his band."

In the manhunt following the Lawrence mas-
sacre, Union troops raided the James-Samuel farm
again, arresting Zerelda. Jesse James was furious. In
the spring of 1864, at the age of 16, Jesse joined a
guerrilla troop led by Bloody Bill Anderson. Bloody
Bill's men rampaged through Missouri and Kansas,
attacking Union posts and shooting Union sympathizers. Young Jesse became adept at galloping into
clashes with his horse's reins in his teeth and
revolvers in both hands. Bloody Bill admired Jesse
and called him "the keenest and cleanest fighter in
the command."

Jesse was wounded in the chest on August 10,
1864, while trying to steal a saddle. He escaped and
was taken to an inn operated by his relatives, Mary
and John Mimms. There, Jesse was nursed back to
health by his cousin Zerelda (Zee) Mimms. After
two months, he recovered from his chest injury and
rejoined Bloody Bill's band.

By then, however, Confederate troops and guer-

Confederate General Robert E. Lee's surrender to Union forces at Appomattox Court House, Virginia, in April 1865 effectively ended the Civil War. However, some Southerners continued fighting for the next several months—among them Jesse James.

rilla units had begun to suffer serious defeats. Bloody Bill Anderson was killed in late 1864, and William Quantrill died from a bullet wound in 1865. The Civil War officially ended on April 9, 1865, when Confederate general Robert E. Lee surrendered to Union general Ulysses S. Grant in Appomattox Court House, Virginia.

Jesse James was certain that he and his gang could elude the law. He was so confident, in fact, that he brought a photographer to their hideout in a Missouri cave to take this picture.

A Life of Crime

After General Lee surrendered, one by one, Confederate armies and guerrilla units gave up. In June 1865, Jesse James and a small group of bushwhackers rode into Lexington, Missouri, to turn themselves in. A band of Union soldiers saw them and opened fire. Jesse's horse was killed and Jesse was hit in the chest. One of the bushwhackers quickly pulled the wounded Jesse up behind him and raced away with his companions. Jesse had a hole in his lung and could not stay on the horse. He dismounted and crawled into the woods.

A Confederate sympathizer found Jesse, took him home, and got him medical care. Though badly hurt, Jesse was taken to a farm in Nebraska, where his mother and stepfather were staying. Jesse thought he was dying, and he begged his mother to take him back to Missouri. In August 1865, Zerelda took her son on a boat trip down the Missouri River. As before, Jesse was taken to the Mimmses' inn, where he was nursed by his cousin Zee Mimms. Jesse and Zee fell in love and vowed to marry some day.

Jesse and his mother eventually returned to Kearney. As Jesse *recuperated*, his family worked hard to rebuild their farm. Meanwhile, Frank and Jesse James visited with friends, including Cole Younger and his brothers Bob, John, and James. The former guerrillas told stories about their wartime deeds and talked about their hatred of the Union. As bushwhackers, they had learned to strike suddenly and forcefully and to outfox their enemies. They decided to use these skills to rob a bank owned by hated Northerners—the Clay County Savings Bank in Liberty, Missouri, about 12 miles from Kearney.

Frank James and the rest of Quantrill's band surrendered on July 26, 1865. Union officials made the guerrillas pledge allegiance to the United States, then released them. Frank returned to Kearney, Missouri, to be reunited with his family.

On Tuesday afternoon, February 13, 1866, a group of men dressed like Union soldiers rode up to the bank. Two men dismounted and went inside. The head cashier, Greenup Bird, and his son, William, were working. The men drew their revolvers. They forced the Birds into the bank's vault, filled an empty sack with about $60,000 in gold, silver, currency, and bonds, and raced out.

As the robbers rode away, the Birds hurried out of the bank and raised the alarm. The outlaws shouted and fired wildly as they charged down the street, killing a young man named George Wymore.

No one knows exactly who participated in the Liberty bank heist. Historians believe 18-year-old Jesse James—still recovering from his chest wound—

helped plan the robbery, and that Frank James, the Younger brothers, and others carried it out. Hence, the James-Younger Gang was born. The James and Younger boys formed the hub of the group, and other bandits went along on different jobs. In time, Jesse James–who was clever at planning strategy and choosing targets–became the leader.

After they struck the Liberty bank, Jesse James and his gang robbed banks in several other Missouri towns. Though many *posses* pursued them, the gang members were not caught. They knew the territory well and were able to hide out at the homes of friends and relatives.

The James-Younger Gang used guerrilla tactics to rob banks. They rode into town in small groups to keep from attracting attention. After the robbery, the outlaws bolted away, screeching rebel yells and firing into the air to terrorize the townsfolk. They then split up again to avoid capture.

Soon, Missouri was too dangerous for the bandits, so they moved their operations elsewhere. On March 20, 1868, the James-Younger Gang robbed a bank in Russellville, Kentucky. The outlaws netted between $9,000 and $14,000. A posse tracked the bandits down. Lawmen killed a gunslinger named Oliver

Shepherd and arrested his brother George, but the James and Younger boys got away.

On December 7, 1869, Jesse James and his gang robbed the Daviess County Savings Bank in Gallatin, Missouri. Jesse murdered the bank's owner, Captain John Sheets, in the mistaken belief that Sheets had been in the troop that killed Bloody Bill Anderson. As the bandits galloped away, the townsfolk opened fire. Jesse's horse went wild and the outlaw fell off. His foot was caught in the stirrup, and he was dragged down the street. Jesse managed to free himself, and he mounted behind Frank and rode away. On the outskirts of town, the outlaws stole another horse and headed home.

The senseless murder of Captain Sheets touched off a vast manhunt, with an offer of $3,000 for the capture of the killer. Jesse's abandoned horse was traced to the James-Samuel farm in Clay County. Although a posse surrounded the farm, the James boys were ready. They dashed out of their stable on horseback, jumped a fence, and escaped.

The Daviess robbery marked a turning point. The authorities now had evidence to publicly denounce Frank and Jesse James as criminals. The James boys became fugitives from justice.

This famous photo has appeared in numerous books and articles about the James-Younger Gang. It purports to show Jesse and Frank James seated in front of Cole and Bob Younger. Actually, the photo is a phony; it was taken in Davenport, Iowa, in the winter of 1901 with studio props. Many people have been fascinated by the adventures of the gang, even though Jesse and the others were committing ruthless robberies.

FOLK HEROES

When the authorities publicly accused Frank and Jesse James of committing a string of bank robberies, the James boys became folk heroes. Their greatest fan and defender was a newspaperman, Major John Newman Edwards. Edwards was a former Confederate officer who helped found the *Kansas City Times* in Kansas City, Missouri. When the James brothers were accused of robbing the Daviess County Savings Bank, the *Times* printed a letter signed by Jesse James—though historians believe most of Jesse's letters were written by Edwards himself. The letter said: "Governor, when I think I can get a fair trial I will surrender to the civil authorities of Missouri. But I will never surrender to be mobbed by a set of bloodthirsty **poltroons**."

Many letters attributed to Jesse James were published over the years. The letters, as well as articles written by Edwards, said that Frank and Jesse James had become outlaws because of their mistreatment during and after the Civil War. Edwards wrote that Jesse James was a hero of the Confederacy because he struck back at rich, corrupt Northern businessmen who cheated Southerners. According to Edwards, Jesse James was a sort of "Robin Hood," who stole from the rich to help the poor.

This was not true—Jesse and his gang kept their loot and spent it on themselves, not the poor. Nevertheless, many Missouri residents agreed that Jesse James was a hero. They hid Jesse and his band in barns and fields, gave them food, and helped them evade the law for many years.

While waiting for lawmen to give up their search

for the desperadoes that robbed the Daviess County Savings Bank, Frank and Jesse drifted around Missouri, Texas, Arkansas, Nebraska, Kentucky, and possibly the East Coast. They lived on their stolen funds. Then, on June 3, 1871, Jesse's gang struck a bank in Corydon, Iowa. At the time of the robbery, the townspeople were in the local church-yard, listening to a politician's speech. The James boys enjoyed being famous and liked to bolster their reputations. Thus, as they rode out of town, Frank James stopped at the churchyard to announce that the bank had just been robbed. The crowd hushed him, thinking it was a joke. The residents found out later, of course, that the bank *had* just been robbed.

The James and Younger boys continued to rob banks, and in 1872, they were accused of holding up the Kansas City Fair. On the afternoon of September 26, three men with bandanas over their faces rode through a huge crowd to the fair's ticket booth. The bandits grabbed a metal box holding about $1,000 in admission fees. A fair employee tried to take the box back, and during the scuffle, a little girl was wounded in the leg. The next day, the *Kansas City Times* called the robbery the "Most

Desperate and Daring Robbery of the Age." John Newman Edwards wrote an *editorial,* in which he said he regretted the little girl's injury but applauded the holdup as an act of resistance against Washington politicians. Historians think this robbery, and some others credited to the James-Younger Gang, may have been the work of "copycat" outlaws.

In 1873, the James-Younger Gang began robbing railroads. On July 21, 1873, they held up their first train, in Adair, Iowa. The bandits knew that the train—on the Chicago, Rock Island, and Pacific Railroad—carried a large shipment of gold. To stop the train, the outlaws pulled out a rail close to the station. The locomotive toppled over, killing the engineer, John Rafferty. The bandits then donned masks and charged into the train. The gunslingers were appalled to discover that the train's wealth was not precious coins, but heavy gold and silver bars that could not be carried away on horseback. The outlaws got only a couple of thousand dollars from the train's safe before they made their escape.

When news of the train robbery got out, many people applauded the James boys. Farmers hated the railroad barons, who bought up valuable land

When the James-Younger Gang started robbing trains, beginning in the summer of 1873, their popularity grew because many people hated the large, wealthy railroad companies. Also, stories began to circulate that the gang only robbed rich people, not poor farmers or working men.

and charged high rates for shipping goods. The railroad tycoons were incensed by the robbery and frustrated by the inability of local sheriffs and posses to catch the outlaws. Railroad owners met with

Frequent stage and train robberies by the James-Younger Gang made people afraid to travel through the state. "The damage inflicted upon Missouri [by the gang] is beyond calculation," read an editorial in one New York newspaper. "When a traveler got into a Missouri train he did so with the same feeling that a man has when going into battle—with little expectation of getting through alive."

bank owners, and they decided to hire the best lawmen in the country—the Pinkerton National Detective Agency. Pinkerton detectives had caught many criminals across the country, including forgers, pickpockets, safecrackers, diamond thieves, and *embezzlers*. The Pinkerton lawmen chasing the James-Younger Gang, however, had huge problems.

First, they got no assistance from local residents, who viewed the detectives as hired guns of hated corporations. Second, the Pinkertons knew little about Missouri, and they were not familiar with the appearance, habits, or tactics of Jesse's band.

Lawmen could do little to slow down Jesse and his gang, who soon added stagecoaches to their list of targets. On January 15, 1874, a stage carrying 14 wealthy passengers rumbled toward the health resort of Hot Springs, Arkansas. Near Sulphur Creek, five gunmen with handkerchiefs over their faces jumped out and ordered the driver to stop. The bandits then took the passengers' money, watches, and jewelry. They unhitched the coach's horses, chased them off, and made their getaway.

After the robbery, stories circulated that one of the passengers had told the bandits he was a Confederate veteran, and that Cole Younger had returned the man's watch and money bag. This incident led to tales about the James-Younger Gang never robbing Southerners. This was not true. Many of the gang's victims were from the South.

The bandits added to their fame on January 31, 1874, when they held up a train at Gads Hill, Missouri, on the Iron Mountain Railroad. As they

A Pinkerton detective tracking the James-Younger Gang spoke of asking a local lawman to help him: "He said he would ... aid me secretly, but owing to the relatives and sympathizers of these men residing in the country he dared not lend me a hand openly."

robbed the passengers, the outlaws asked to see the hands of the men. If the passengers were "working men"–men whose hands were rough and callused–the outlaws did not take their money; they also did not rob the women.

Moreover, as the gunmen were leaving the train, one of them gave the railroad engineer a written account of the robbery. All the newspapers had to do was fill in the correct amount of money stolen. The outlaws had titled the story, "The Most Daring Robbery on Record."

After the Gad's Hill robbery, the Pinkertons sent a young detective named John Whicher to Liberty, Missouri. Whicher arrived on March 10, 1874, disguised himself as a farmhand, and trekked towards the James-Samuel farm to ask for work. The James brothers got word of the plan and caught the agent. Whicher's body was later found alongside a road near Independence, Missouri, with bullets through his heart and head. A few days later, three Pinkerton agents tried to round up John and James Younger near Osceola, Missouri. The confrontation ended in a gun battle that left two Pinkerton agents and John Younger dead. James Younger and one Pinkerton agent survived.

The Pinkerton tragedies led Missouri newspapers to scoff at law enforcement officials in the state. On March 21, 1874, an editorial in the *St. Louis Republican* read:

> Judges, sheriffs, constables, and the whole machinery of law are either set at defiance [influenced to defy the law] by a gang of villains, or bought or frightened into neutrality. . . . That [such a condition] exists in Missouri is a fact as remarkable as it is outrageous. If the governor of Missouri and the legislature of Missouri are unable to devise ways and means for effectively breaking up these nests of thieves and cut-throats, then let them . . . ask for assistance from the federal government. Anything is better than this tame submission to systematic ***brigandage***.

This photograph of Jesse James was taken in 1874, around the time he was married to Zerelda (Zee) Mimms. Jesse continued his life of crime as the couple started a family. To avoid capture, they told others their family name was Howard. Jesse sometimes went by the name John Davis Howard; other times he called himself Thomas Howard.

THE LEGEND GROWS

Jesse James's marriage added to his legend as a *glamorous* villain. After being engaged for nine years, Jesse and his cousin, Zee Mimms, planned to wed on April 24, 1874. The James and Mimms families gathered at the home of Zee's sister, Lucy Mimms Browder, in Kearney, Missouri. Just before the ceremony, Jesse got word that two lawmen on his trail were racing over from

Liberty, Missouri. The bride was quickly hidden in a feather bed. As soon as the detectives entered the house, Jesse bolted away on his horse, causing the lawmen to chase him. Jesse managed to lose his pursuers, and he hurried back for a quick ceremony.

Jesse later wrote, "[Zee's] devotion to me has never wavered for a moment. You can say that both of us married for love, and that there cannot be any sort of doubt about our marriage being a happy one."

After the wedding, Jesse and Zee honeymooned in Texas for several months. The couple returned to Missouri in August 1874 and made their first home in Kansas City.

Meanwhile, the crimes of the James-Younger Gang led Eastern newspapers to write about "The Bandit State of Missouri." Newspaper articles led people to believe that Missouri was filled with murderous thieves who were allowed to walk free year after year. Missouri's governor, Silas Woodson, became desperate. He offered $10,000 to pay police agents to track the gang down, but the agents had no more luck than previous investigators.

On the night of January 25, 1875, the Pinkertons, again hired by the railroads, made a daring attempt to capture Frank and Jesse James. Having gotten word that the bandits were at the James-Samuel farm in Kearney, Missouri, Pinkerton agents surrounded the house. The agents threw two bombs, made of gunpowder-filled tubes inside burning **gunnysacks**, through the windows. They wanted to set fire to the house and force the occupants to flee.

Jesse's step-father, Dr. Reuben Samuel, extinguished one bomb. He pushed the other bomb into the fireplace, where it exploded. **Shrapnel** shattered Zerelda Samuel's right arm and fatally wounded Jesse's half-brother, eight-year-old Archie Samuel. If Frank and Jesse James were in the house, they escaped. The Pinkertons, seeing the explosion, hurried away.

The people of Missouri were outraged. The *Kansas City Times* wrote, "There is no crime, however dastardly, which merits a retribution as savage and fiendish as the one which these men acting under the semblance of law have perpetrated." On March 8, 1875, the *St. Louis Dispatch* asked for **pardons** for the James-Younger Gang, and other newspapers repeated the request. Pardons were not granted, however. Meanwhile, the James boys took revenge, killing some local men suspected of helping the bombers.

Because Jesse and Zee James were using false names to avoid the law, their children, Mary and Jesse Jr., believed their last name was Howard. Jesse Jr.'s middle name, Edwards, came from Jesse's faithful supporter, Major John Newman Edwards.

The Pinkertons gave up their search for the James-Younger Gang soon after the farmhouse bombing episode. Robert Pinkerton, son of the agency's founder, later said, "I consider Jesse James the worst man, without exception, in America."

Soon the people of Missouri began to develop mixed feelings about the James-Younger Gang. Though many admired the famous gang's courage and daring exploits, people were frightened and horrified by the gang's murderous violence.

After the bombing, Jesse and his wife—using the names John Davis Howard and Josie Howard—moved to the Nashville, Tennessee, area. They rented a house on a hill so they could watch for posses approaching from any direction. To explain his frequent absences from home, Jesse told his neighbors he was a businessman. After a "business trip," Jesse would deliver large sacks of money, jewelry, and other valuables to his wife.

In 1875, Zee gave birth to a son, Jesse Edwards James. Jesse and Zee then moved to Baltimore, Maryland, for a short time before returning to Missouri. In 1878, Zee gave birth to twin boys, Gould and Montgomery. The babies were sickly and died in infancy. In 1879, Zee had a daughter, Mary Susan James.

Jesse James and his gang always wanted money. In 1876, they planned a big heist with several other bandits, including a man named Hobbs Kerry. On July 7 of that year, the gang robbed a Missouri Pacific Railroad train at Rocky Cut, Missouri. They netted about $15,000. Afterward, Hobbs Kerry was arrested by the St. Louis police. He soon confessed to holding up the train and named Jesse James and his gang as accomplices.

After the Rocky Cut train robbery, an accomplice of the James-Younger Gang, Bill Chadwell, suggested that the gang move their operations to his home state of Minnesota. This would prove to be a disastrous move for the outlaws.

PROCLAMATION

OF THE

GOVERNOR OF MISSOURI!

REWARDS

FOR THE ARREST OF

Express and Train Robbers.

STATE OF MISSOURI,}
EXECUTIVE DEPARTMENT.

WHEREAS, It has been made known to me, as the Governor of the State of Missouri, that certain parties, whose names are to me unknown, have confederated and banded themselves together for the purpose of committing robberies and other depredations within this State; and

WHEREAS, Said parties did, on or about the Eighth day of October, 1879, stop a train near Glendale, in the county of Jackson, in said State, and, with force and violence, take, steal and carry away the money and other express matter being carried thereon; and

WHEREAS, On the fifteenth day of July 1881, said parties and their confederates did stop a train upon the line of the Chicago, Rock Island and Pacific Railroad, near Winston, in the County of Daviess, in said State, and, with force and violence, take, steal, and carry away the money and other express matter being carried thereon; and, in perpetration of the robbery last aforesaid, the parties engaged therein did kill and murder one WILLIAM WESTFALL, the conductor of the train, together with one JOHN McCULLOH, who was at the time in the employ of said company, then on said train; and

WHEREAS, FRANK JAMES and JESSE W. JAMES stand indicted in the Circuit Court of said Daviess County, for the murder of JOHN W. SHEETS, and the parties engaged in the robberies and murders aforesaid have fled from justice and have absconded and secreted themselves;

NOW, THEREFORE, in consideration of the premises, and in lieu of all other rewards heretofore offered for the arrest or conviction of the parties aforesaid, or either of them, by any person or corporation, I, THOMAS T. CRITTENDEN, Governor of the State of Missouri, do hereby offer a reward of five thousand dollars ($5,000.00) for the arrest and conviction of each person participating in either of the robberies or murders aforesaid, excepting the said FRANK JAMES and JESSE W. JAMES; and for the arrest and delivery of said

FRANK JAMES and JESSE W. JAMES,

and each or either of them, to the sheriff of said Daviess County, I hereby offer a reward of five thousand dollars, ($5,000.00,) and for the conviction of either of the parties last aforesaid of participation in either of the murders or robberies above mentioned, I hereby offer a further reward of five thousand dollars, ($5,000.00.)

IN TESTIMONY WHEREOF, I have hereunto set my hand and caused to be affixed the Great Seal of the State of Missouri. Done

[SEAL.]   at the City of Jefferson on this 25th day of July, A. D. 1881.

THOS. T. CRITTENDEN.

By the Governor:

MICH'L K. McGRATH, Sec'y of State.

BURCH & PEMBROOK, STATE PRINTERS, JEFFERSON CITY, MO.

This "wanted" poster offers $5,000 for the arrest of Frank and Jesse James, and an additional $5,000 if the brothers are convicted.

THE NORTHFIELD DISASTER

In the summer of 1876, the James-Younger Gang went north. Jesse James and his gang planned to rob a bank in Northfield, Minnesota, a community containing many immigrants from Norway and Sweden. On the morning of September 7, 1876, eight bandits–Frank and Jesse James; Cole, James, and Bob Younger; Bill Chadwell; Clell Miller; and Charlie Pitts–climbed on their horses and rode toward town. Their long linen coats hid guns and ammunition belts.

Jesse James, Charlie Pitts, and Bob Younger approached the bank first. They slid off their horses and sat down on boxes lying in front of a store. Shortly afterward, Cole Younger and Clell Miller rode in from the opposite direction and dismounted. Jesse and his two companions stood up and entered the bank, leaving Miller and Cole Younger standing outside as lookouts.

The robbery immediately started to go wrong. The men hanging around the bank attracted the townspeople's attention, and J. S. Allen, a local merchant, tried to go inside. Clell Miller grabbed Allen and told him to get back. The merchant pulled away and ran down the street, shouting "Get your guns, boys. They are robbing the bank." Other people soon chimed in, and the street filled with shouts.

Clell Miller and Cole Younger began riding up and down the street. They were soon joined by James Younger, Bill Chadwell, and Frank James, who had been waiting at the edge of town. Meanwhile, the residents of Northfield left the streets, closed their shops and offices, and got their guns. Gunfire was exchanged, with the Northfield citizens firing from windows, rooftops, and sheltered corners. A Northfield man named Nicholas Gustavson was fatally wounded, and two outlaws—Bill Chadwell and Clell Miller—were killed.

The robbers inside the bank also had trouble. The bank employees refused to open the safe, which, unknown to the gunmen, was not locked. The outlaws struck Joseph Heywood, the cashier, and knocked him down. Another bank employee, A. E. Bunker, rushed to the door. He was shot by Pitts but made it outside. In the street, one of the outlaws shouted to his *comrades* in the bank, saying, "They are killing all our men!" As the bandits ran out, one of them shot Heywood in the head.

The *desperadoes* made their getaway amidst a hail of gunfire. In the end, six—the three Younger brothers; Frank and Jesse James; and Charlie Pitts—escaped into the countryside. All of the Youngers were badly wounded, and Frank was shot in the leg. The bandits got only $26.70.

Telegraph messages raced through Minnesota, relaying the news that the Northfield bank robbers were wounded and on the run. Farmers, townspeople, and lawmen from all over the state organized posses to bring them down.

These men were members of the posse that killed Charlie Pitts and captured Cole, Jim, and Bob Younger after the James Gang's failed holdup of the Northfield bank in 1876. The successful escape of Frank and Jesse James enhanced their legend. A Sedalia, Missouri, newspaper later wrote: "They ran the gauntlet of Minnesota and Dakota for a distance of 490 miles, and the wildest exploits . . . will not compare with this bold ride for life."

The James boys had counted on Bill Chadwell, who came from Minnesota, to guide them through the state—but he was dead. The bandits blundered around, finally locating an abandoned farmhouse near Mankato, Minnesota. They holed up there for a day to rest. Meanwhile, search parties spread out, guarding every possible escape route.

The gang split up. Frank and Jesse James went one way, and the Younger brothers and Charlie Pitts another. In mid-September, the James brothers made it to the Dakota Territory and forced a doctor to treat Frank's wounded leg. The Younger brothers and Pitts also tried to escape, but they were trapped by lawmen in Minnesota. In an exchange of gunfire, Pitts was killed and the Youngers surrendered.

The Youngers were brought to the county jail in Faribault, Minnesota, to await trial. They pled guilty to the murders of Heywood and Gustavson, to attacking townspeople with deadly weapons, and to attempted bank robbery. The Youngers were sentenced to life in prison and locked up in the Minnesota State Penitentiary in Stillwater.

For three years after the Northfield disaster, Frank and Jesse James avoided capture by moving their families from city to city in Tennessee and the Midwest. Jesse, using the alias John Davis Howard, tried to live a normal life. He and Zee gave occasional parties and attended church socials.

Though Jesse James's gang was shattered—with the Youngers in prison and other gang members jailed or dead—he eventually returned to a life of crime.

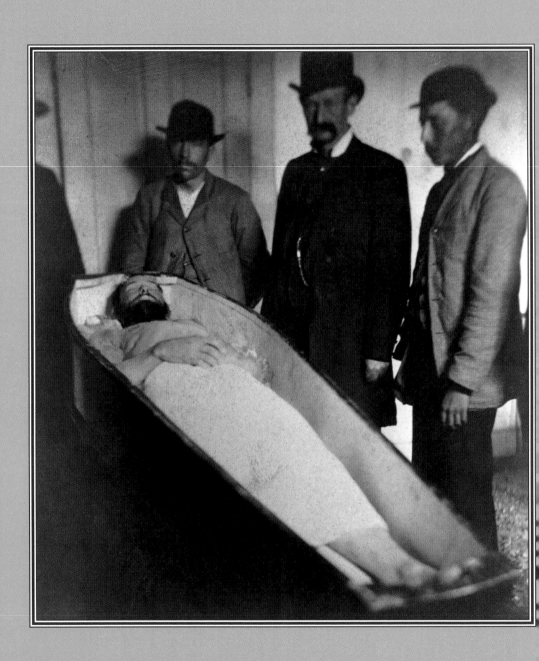

Frank James (center) gazes sadly on the body of his brother Jesse, shot down in his home in April 1882. Jesse was just 34 years old when he was killed; he had spent more than half his life as an outlaw.

The End of Jesse James

After the Northfield affair, Jesse James lived on money stolen in previous robberies. Over time, though, Jesse gambled much of his money away and piled up large debts. Needing funds, Jesse once again took up a life of crime.

Most of Jesse James's most loyal comrades had been captured or killed during the Northfield robbery, so

Jesse recruited new gang members. Jesse's new gang included Ed Miller (Clell Miller's brother), Wood Hite (Jesse's cousin), Tucker Bassham, Bill Ryan, and Dick Liddill.

On the night of October 8, 1879, Jesse's new gang robbed the Chicago and Alton Railroad in the town of Glendale, Missouri. The bandits wrecked the train station's telegraph equipment and forced the agent to signal the train to halt. They then piled rocks on the tracks in case the engineer refused to stop. The raid on the train paid well. The gang made off with $6,000 from the safe.

The robbery rekindled publicity about Jesse James just as politicians were preparing for the 1880 election. The Democratic candidate for governor was Thomas T. Crittenden. He promised to bring down Jesse James and his band. By 1880, most Missouri residents no longer considered Jesse James a hero out to avenge the South. Jesse and his gang now seemed to want only money and fame, and Missouri citizens wanted them stopped. Crittenden was elected governor.

The James boys went on committing crimes. On July 15, 1881, Jesse's gang robbed a train on the Chicago, Rock Island, and Pacific Railroad near

Gallatin, Missouri. They knew that twice a week the train brought thousands of dollars to a bank in Gallatin. During the heist, two men were shot. The gang had robbed the wrong train, however, and got away with only about $700.

Governor Crittenden was outraged. He met with the state's railroad executives, who pledged a total of $50,000 for the capture of the James Gang. The governor offered $10,000 apiece for the arrest and conviction of Frank and Jesse James.

In spite of the rewards, the James Gang continued to rob trains. However, Jesse began to suspect everyone of plotting against him, even his own men. After Jesse had an argument with Ed Miller, Miller disappeared. The outlaw's body was later found beside a country road with a bullet in the head. Historians think Jesse killed Miller, perhaps fearing Miller was about to turn him in. It was about this time that Jesse began always carrying his revolvers.

In late 1881, Jesse James moved his family to the thriving town of St. Joseph, Missouri. In a stable attached to their house, Jesse kept two horses. One was always saddled—ready for a quick getaway.

Jesse's new gang soon began to fall apart. Tucker Bassham was arrested after bragging about his involvement with the James Gang. He confessed to his part in the Glendale train robbery and made a deal to testify against Bill Ryan, who had also been caught. Bassham gave evidence during Ryan's trial and revealed Jesse James's role in the robberies. Ryan was convicted and sentenced to 25 years in prison. Bassham received a pardon and quickly left the area.

According to the prosecutor, William Wallace, "The jury which convicted Ryan broke the backbone of outlawry in the state of Missouri. Thousands of mouths that had been locked by fear were opened." People were now willing to testify against Jesse James and his gang.

Jesse went on planning robberies, and he recruited new bandits, including Bob and Charlie Ford. At the end of 1881, Dick Liddill and the Ford brothers had an argument with Jesse's cousin, Wood Hite. Gunfire was exchanged and Hite was killed. The outlaws quickly hid Hite's body. They were afraid that Jesse would kill them when he found out about his cousin's death. Lured by the reward on Jesse's head, the bandits made a deal with Governor Crittenden. Liddill agreed to testify against Jesse James. Bob and Charlie Ford had other plans.

Bob Ford expected fame and reward as the killer of Jesse James. Instead, he and his brother were arrested and charged with murder. Although he was pardoned by the governor, Ford was despised for shooting Jesse James from behind. He became known as the "dirty little coward that shot Mr. Howard."

On April 3, 1882, while the Fords were guests at Jesse James's house in St. Joseph, Missouri, Bob Ford shot Jesse through the back of the head. Though the public wanted Jesse James stopped, people were outraged at this cold-blooded killing. The Ford brothers were arrested and charged with murder. They claimed their deal with Governor Crittenden was to bring in Jesse James dead or alive, but the governor said his offer was only for the capture of the outlaw.

On April 17, 1881, Bob and Charlie Ford pled guilty to murder and were sentenced to hang. Governor Crittenden immediately gave them full pardons, and they walked away free men. The governor's action led people to believe he had plotted to kill Jesse James, and Crittenden's political career was soon over.

Jesse James was buried near his mother's home in Kearney, Missouri. Zerelda Samuel kept her son's grave decorated with flowers. For years afterward, tourists visited Jesse's grave and paid a fee to hear Zerelda tell stories about her sons.

After Jesse's death, Frank James wanted to give up his life of crime. In 1882, John Newman Edwards negotiated Frank's surrender with Governor Crittenden. On October 5, 1882, Frank gave himself up and was charged with several of the gang's crimes. He was tried and acquitted of all charges.

On May 4, 1884, Charlie Ford, sick with *tuberculosis*, shot himself in the chest. Bob Ford tried to become famous as the "the man who shot Jesse James," but his reputation as a

After Jesse James's death, Major John Newman Edwards wrote in his newspaper: "There was never a more cowardly and unnecessary murder committed in all America than this murder of Jesse James.... He was in the heart of a large city. One word would have summoned 500 armed men for his capture or extermination.... It was his blood the bloody wretches were after."

"back shooter" did not sit well with people. On June 8, 1892, Bob Ford was shot and killed by a gunman in Creede, Colorado.

In 1889, Bob Younger died in prison from tuberculosis. Cole and James Younger received paroles in 1901 and left the Minnesota state prison. James Younger, still suffering from wounds received during the Northfield robbery, committed suicide in 1902. Cole Younger went on to form a traveling show with Frank James, called the "Great Cole Younger and Frank James Historical Wild West." The show—which had fake gunfights, horse stunts, and a fake stagecoach robbery—was not a success. Eventually, Frank James moved back to the James-Samuel farm, where he charged 50 cents per visitor for a tour. He went on to live a quiet life with his family, farming and working at various jobs. He died in 1915 at the age of 72. Cole Younger died a year later.

The James-Samuel house in Kearney is now a tourist attraction that draws thousands of visitors each year. Tourists also visit St. Joseph, Missouri, to attend Jesse James festivals and see the house where Jesse was killed. Despite Jesse James's death, his legend is still very much alive.

CHRONOLOGY

1843 Frank James is born to Robert Sallee James and Zerelda Cole James in Kearney, Missouri, on January 10.

1847 Jesse Woodson James is born on September 5.

1850 Robert James travels to California during the gold rush and dies of pneumonia.

1855 Zerelda James marries Dr. Reuben Samuel.

1861 The Civil War begins.

1862 Frank James joins a Confederate guerrilla troop called Quantrill's Raiders and meets Cole Younger.

1863 General Thomas Ewing orders Confederate sympathizers out of Missouri; Quantrill's Raiders attack Lawrence, Kansas, on August 21.

1864 Jesse James joins Bloody Bill Anderson's guerrilla troop.

1865 The Civil War ends on April 9.

1866 The James-Younger Gang robs the Clay County Savings Bank in Liberty, Missouri, on February 13. Over the next two years, the gang robs banks in Lexington, Savannah, and Richmond, Missouri. During the Richmond robbery, the mayor and two other men are killed.

1869 The James-Younger Gang holds up the Daviess County Savings Bank in Gallatin, Missouri, on December 7. Major John Newman Edwards defends the gang in the *Kansas City Times*.

1873 The James-Younger Gang holds up its first train–the Chicago, Rock Island, and Pacific Railroad–in Adair, Iowa, on July 21. The railroads hire the Pinkerton

National Detective Agency to track down the outlaws.

1874 Jesse James and his gang pull their first stagecoach robbery, near Sulphur Creek, Arkansas, on January 15; in a clash between the Younger brothers and Pinkerton agents, John Younger and two Pinkerton agents are killed; Jesse James and his cousin Zee Mimms are married in Kearney, Missouri, on April 24.

1875 Pinkerton agents bomb the James-Samuel house on January 25, injuring Jesse James's mother, Zerelda, and killing his half-brother Archie.

1876 The James-Younger Gang robs a bank in Northfield, Minnesota, on September 7. Two gang members are killed, and Cole, Bob, and Jim Younger are later captured, convicted, and imprisoned. Frank and Jesse James escape.

1879 Jesse James and a new gang rob the Chicago and Alton Railroad in Glendale, Missouri, on October 8.

1881 The James Gang robs a train on the Chicago, Rock Island, and Pacific Railroad near Gallatin, Missouri, on July 15. The conductor and a passenger are killed.

1882 Bob Ford, with the help of his brother Charlie, kills Jesse James in St. Joseph, Missouri, on April 3.

1882 Frank James gives himself up, is tried for several of the gang's crimes, and is acquitted of all charges.

1995 The body buried in Jesse James' grave is exhumed and tested to determine whether or not it belonged to the legendary outlaw.

GLOSSARY

abolitionist–a person in favor of ending slavery.

accomplice–a partner in crime.

blazoned–widely published and announced.

brigandage–the lawless actions of bandits.

bushwhackers–pro-slavery raiders in the border states during the Civil War.

comrade–a close friend or associate.

desperado–a daring, violent criminal, especially in the Wild West during the 19th century.

editorial–a newspaper article that gives the opinions of the editors or publishers.

embezzler–someone who secretly steals money or property that has been entrusted to his or her care.

exhume–to take out of the grave or tomb.

glamorous–exciting and appealing.

guerrilla–a person who engages in irregular warfare, such as harassment and sabotage, especially as part of an independent unit.

gunnysack–a bag made of coarse, heavy fabric, such as burlap.

incense–to make extremely angry.

infamy–having a bad reputation.

jayhawkers–pro-abolition raiders in the border states during the Civil War.

outlaw–a lawless person, or a fugitive from the law.

pardon–to forgive someone for committing crimes.

pneumonia–a disease of the lungs caused by infection.

poltroon–a coward.

posse–a group of citizens organized by the sheriff or local lawman to hunt down escaped or fleeing criminals.

prospector–a person who explores an area looking for mineral deposits, such as gold.

recuperate–to rest in order to regain health and strength.

secede–to withdraw from a country or political organization.

shrapnel–fragments of a bomb, mine, or shell.

tuberculosis–a serious, contagious lung disease, usually fatal before the discovery of antibiotics in the 20th century.

vigilant–alert and watchful.

Further Reading

Brant, Marley. *Jesse James: The Man and the Myth.* New York: Berkley Books, 1998.

Bruns, Roger A. *The Bandit: From Jesse James to Pretty Boy Floyd.* New York: Crown Publishers, Inc., 1995.

Bruns, Roger A. *Jesse James: Legendary Outlaw.* Springfield, N.J.: Enslow Publishers, 1998.

Green, Carl R. and William R. Sanford. *Outlaws and Lawmen of the Wild West: Jesse James.* Springfield, N.J.: Enslow Publishers, 1992.

James, Stella Frances. *In the Shadow of Jesse James.* San Francisco: The Revolver Press, 1989.

Newmans, Evans. *The True Story of the Notorious Jesse James: A Biography.* Hicksville, N.Y.: Exposition Press, 1976.

Ross, James R. *I, Jesse James.* California: Dragon Publishing Corp., 1988.

Stiles, T. J. *Jesse James.* New York: Chelsea House Publishers, 1994.

Triplett, Frank. *The Life, Times, and Treacherous Death of Jesse James.* Chicago: The Swallow Press, 1970.

Yeatman, Ted P. *Frank and Jesse James: The Story Behind the Legend.* Nashville, Tenn.: Cumberland House, 2000.

Picture Credits

DR. BARBARA SAFFER, a former college instructor, holds Ph.D. degrees in biology and geology. She has written numerous books for young people about science, geography, and exploration. She lives in Birmingham, Alabama, with her family.